Gnome
Coloring Book

Aryla Publishing 2021

978-1-912675-95-1

www.arylapublishing.com

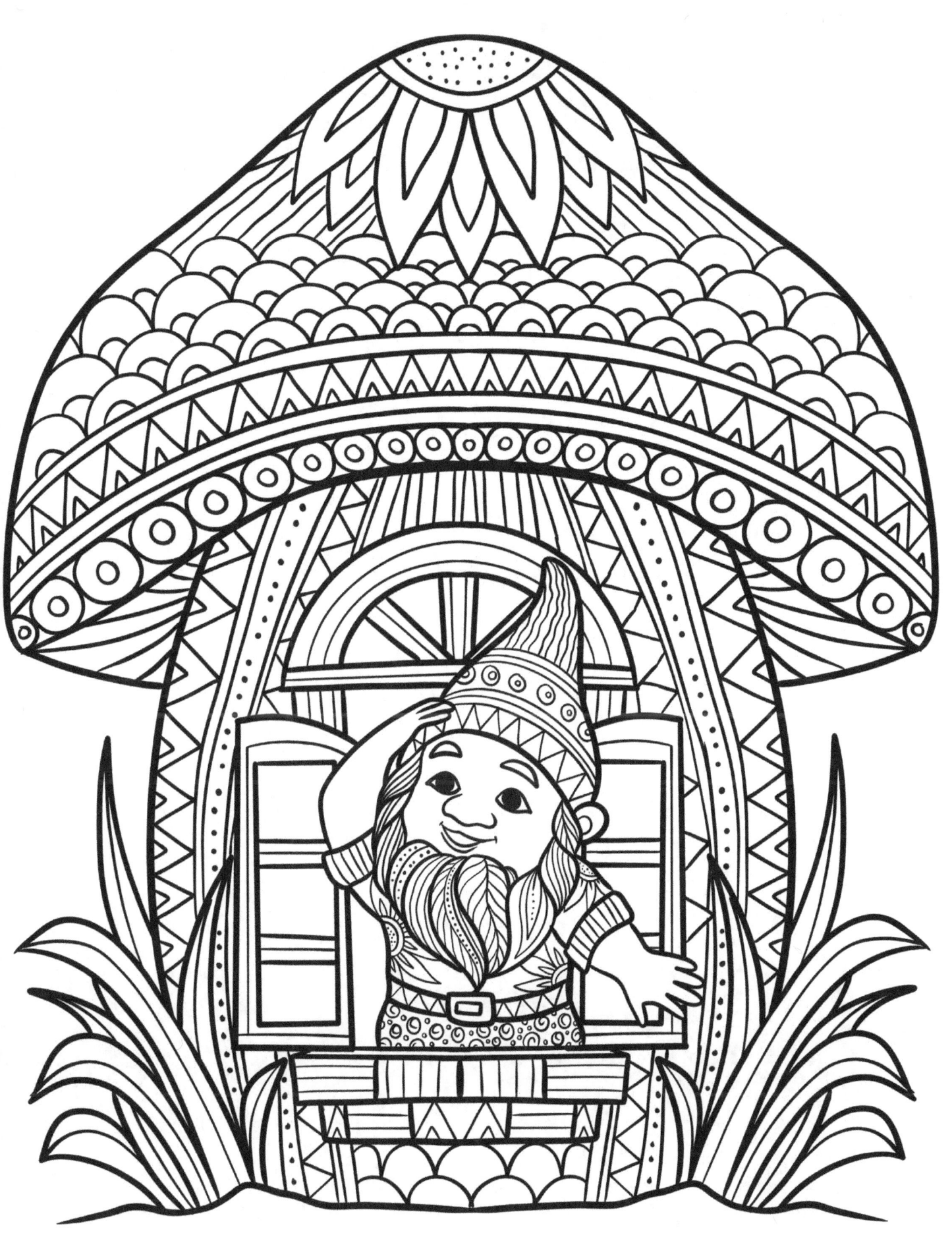

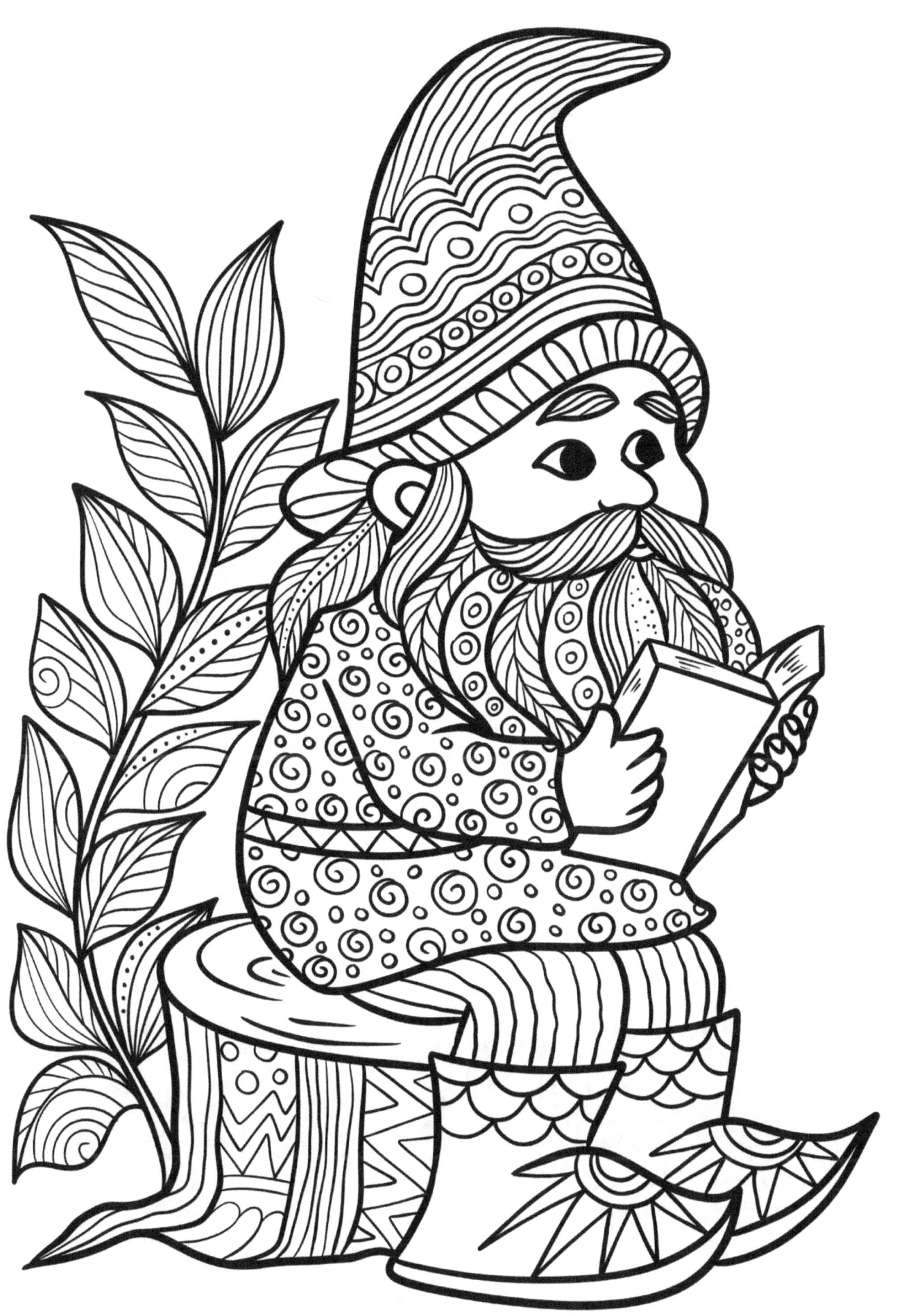

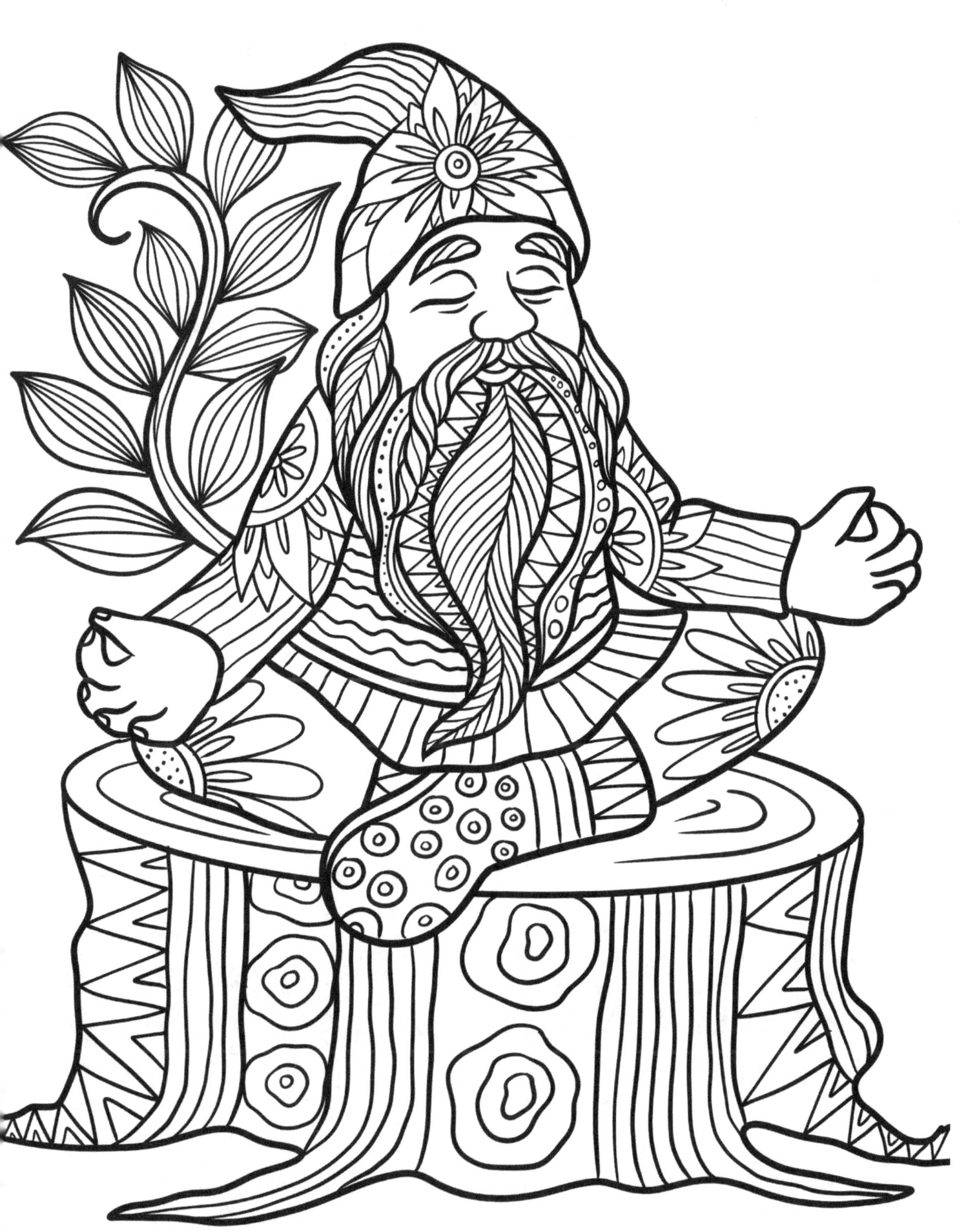

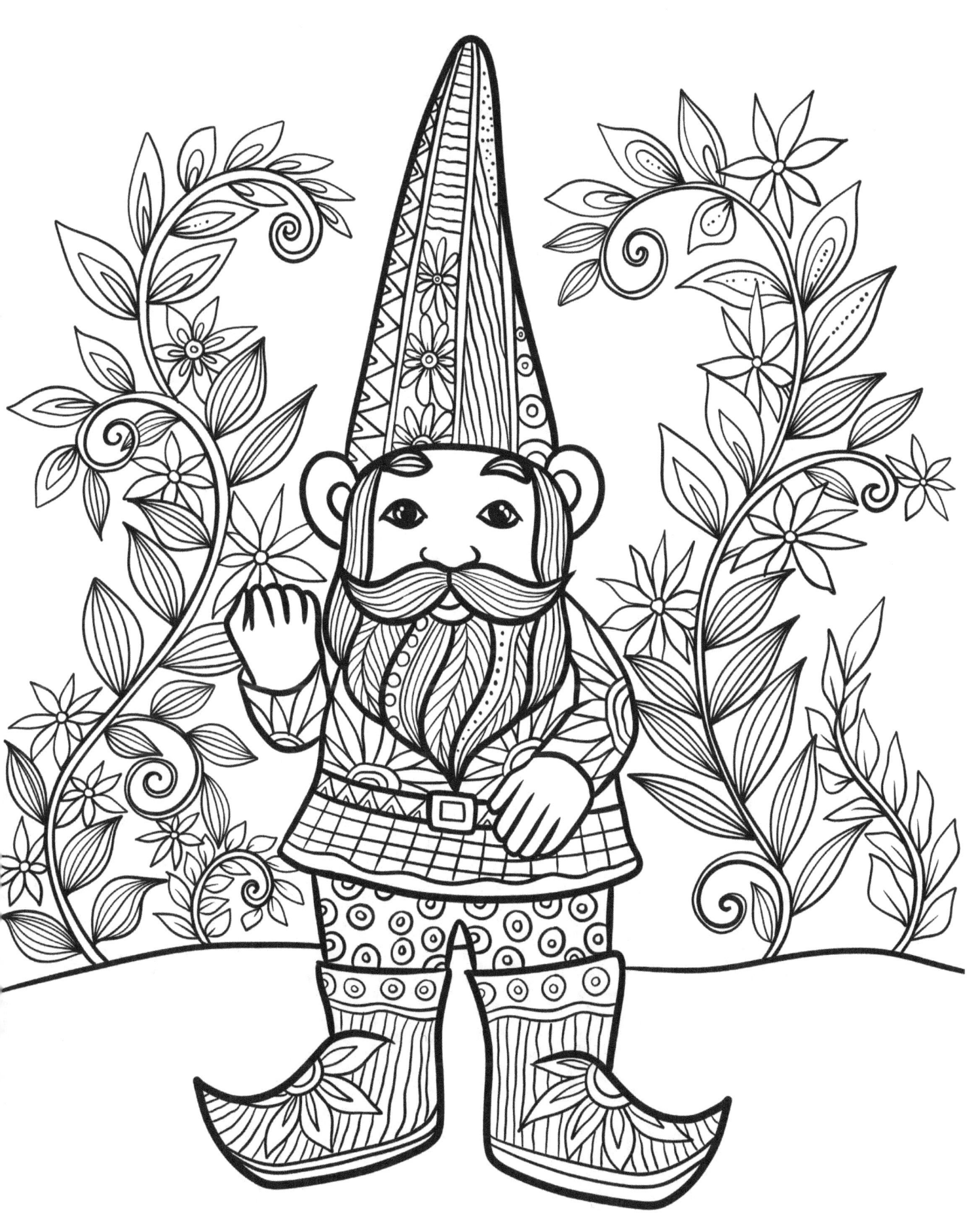

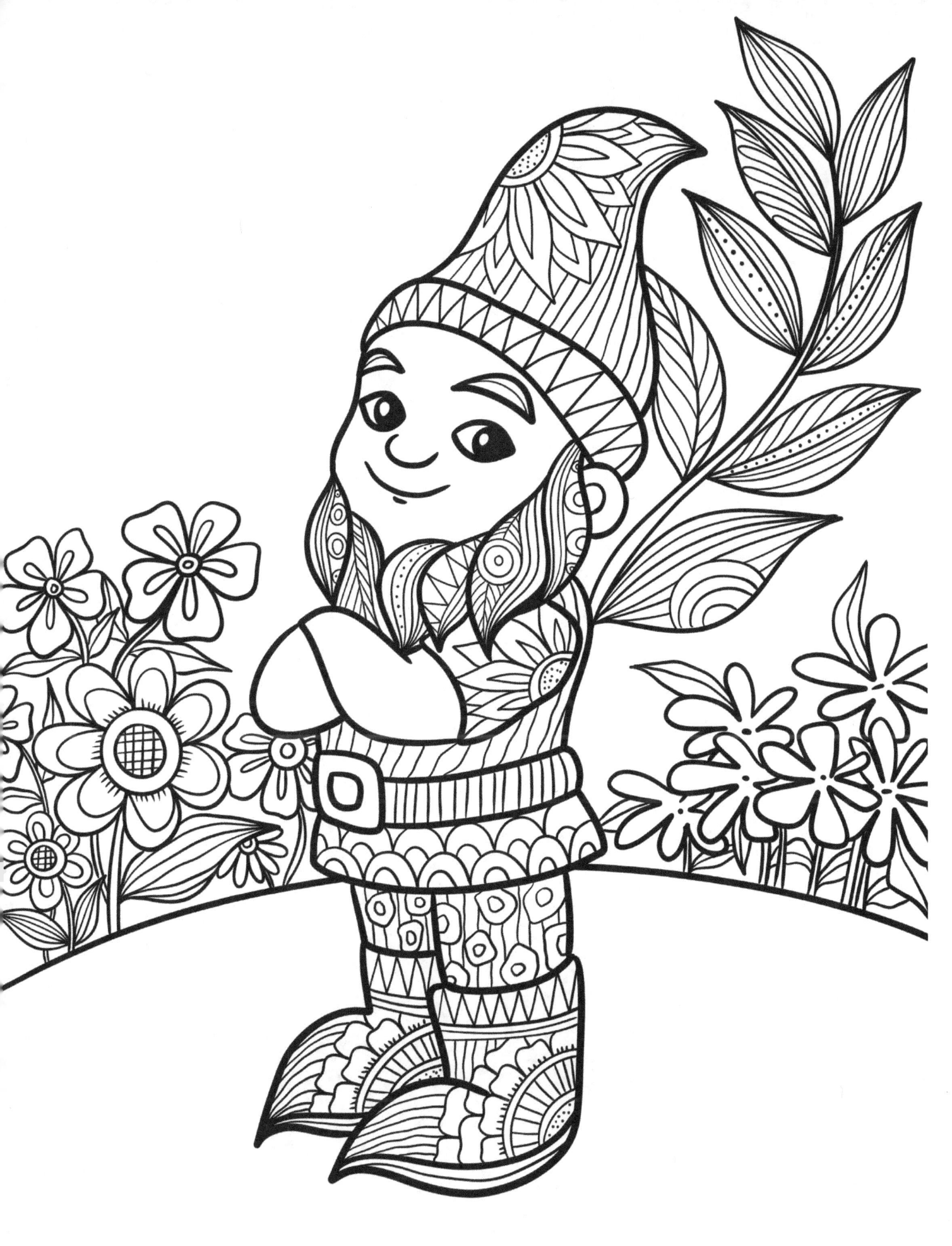

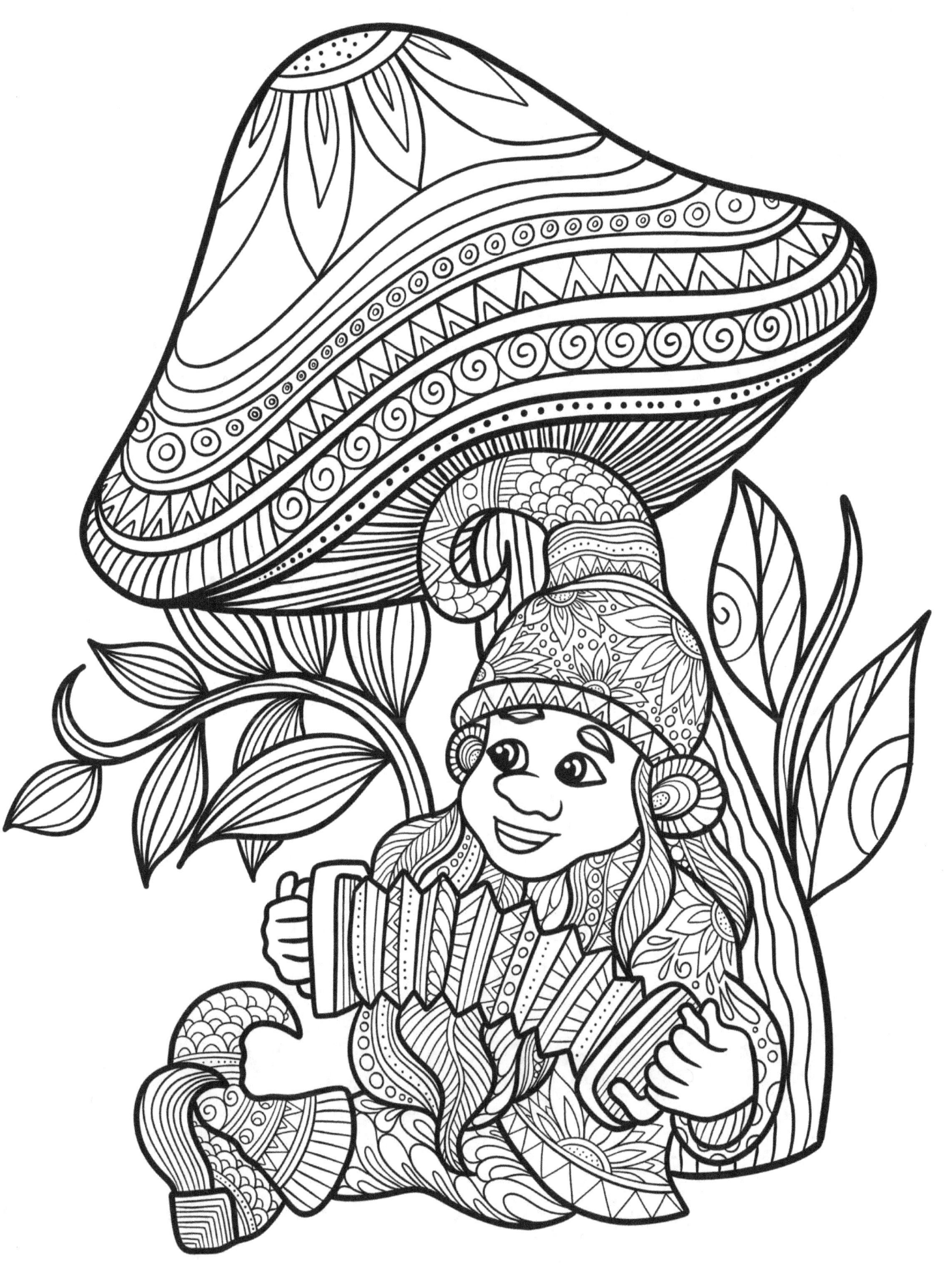

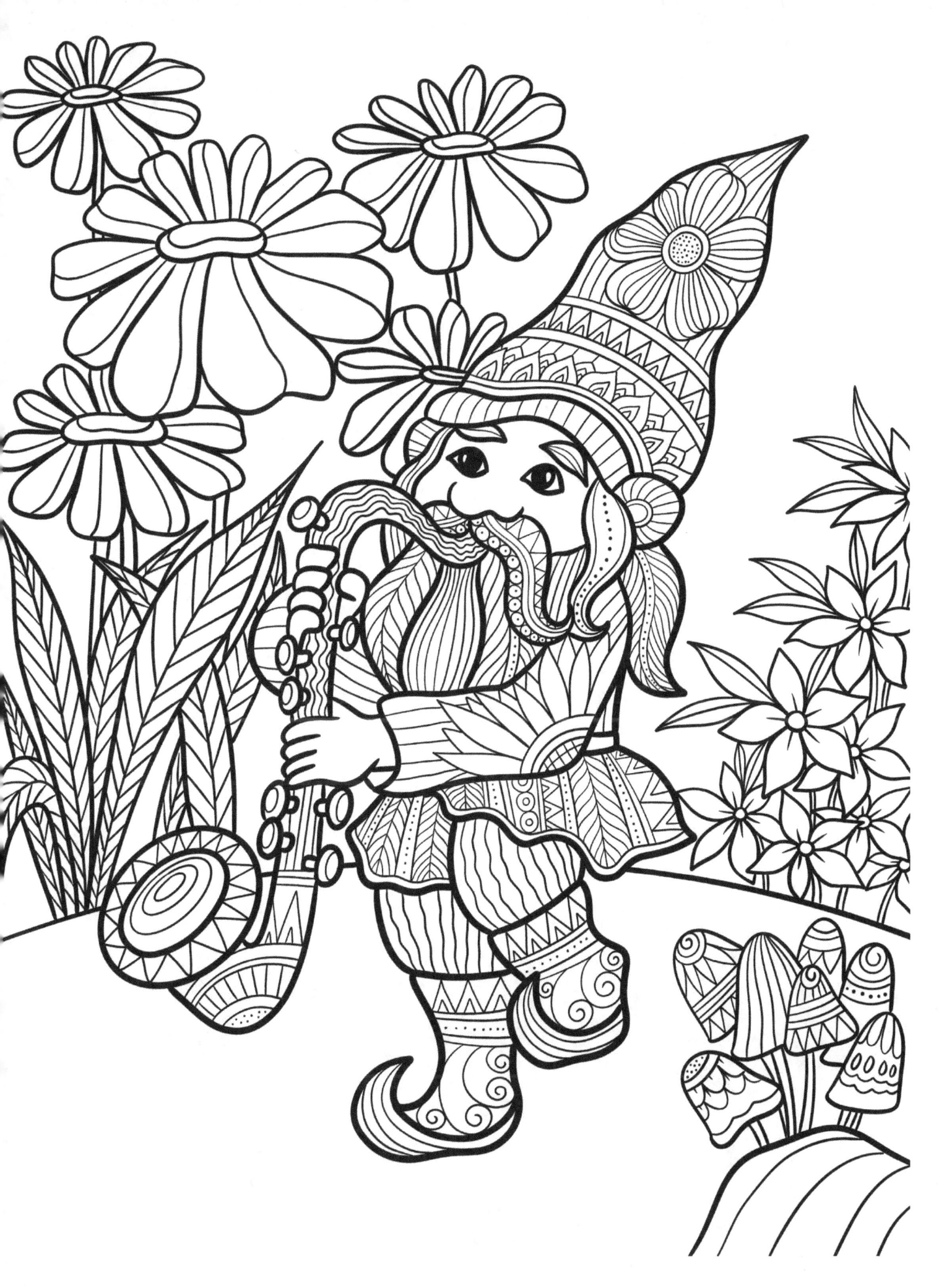

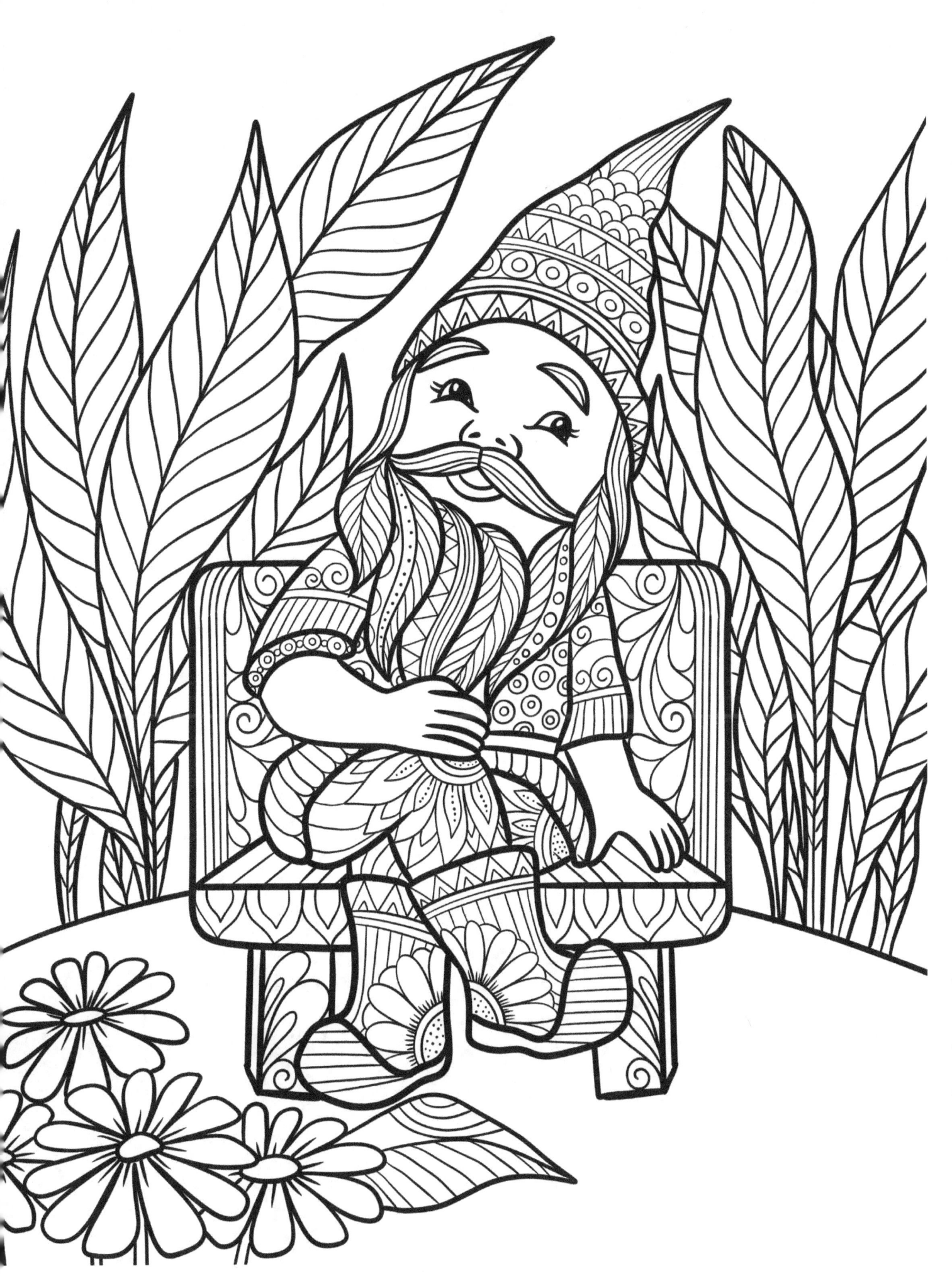

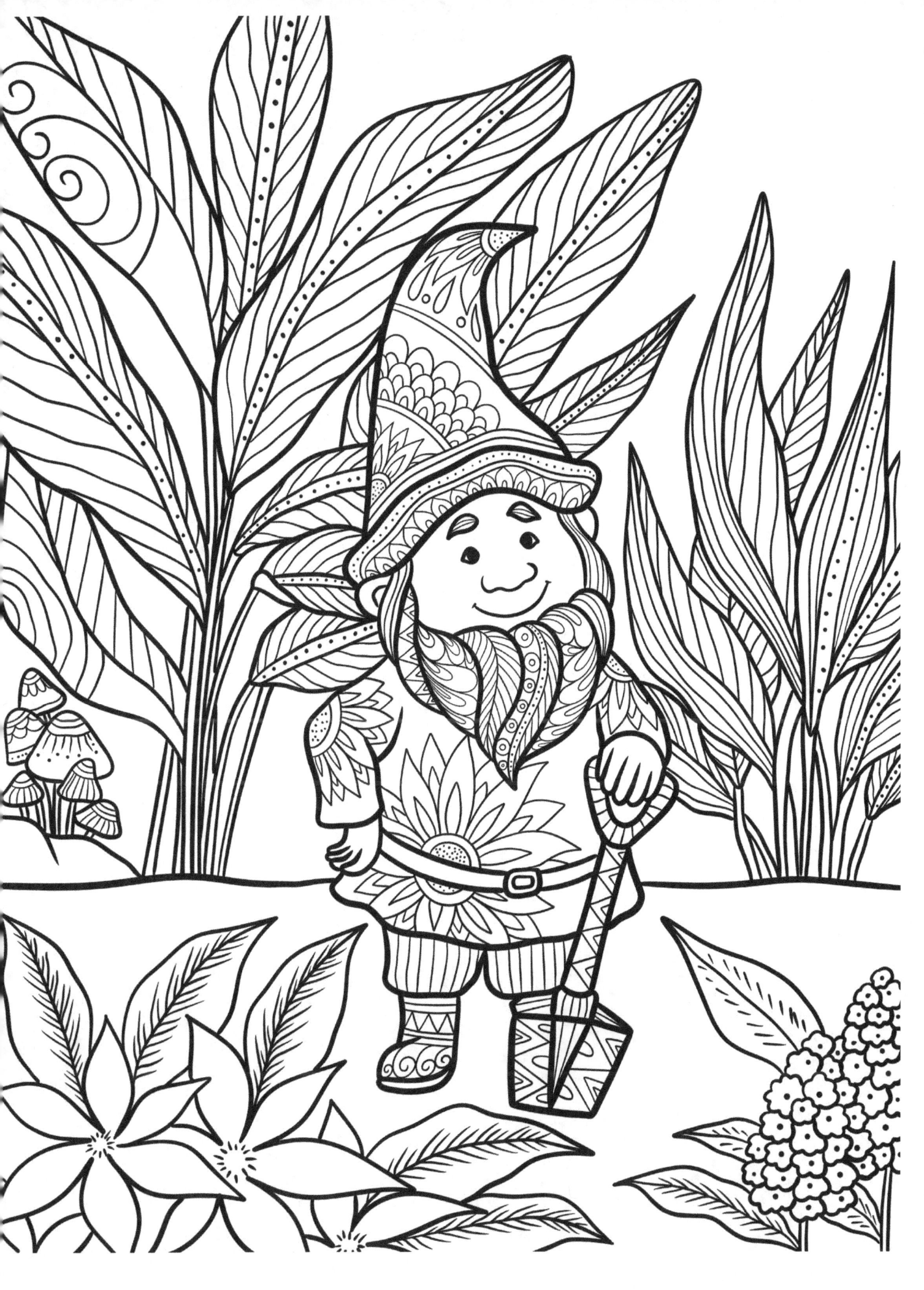

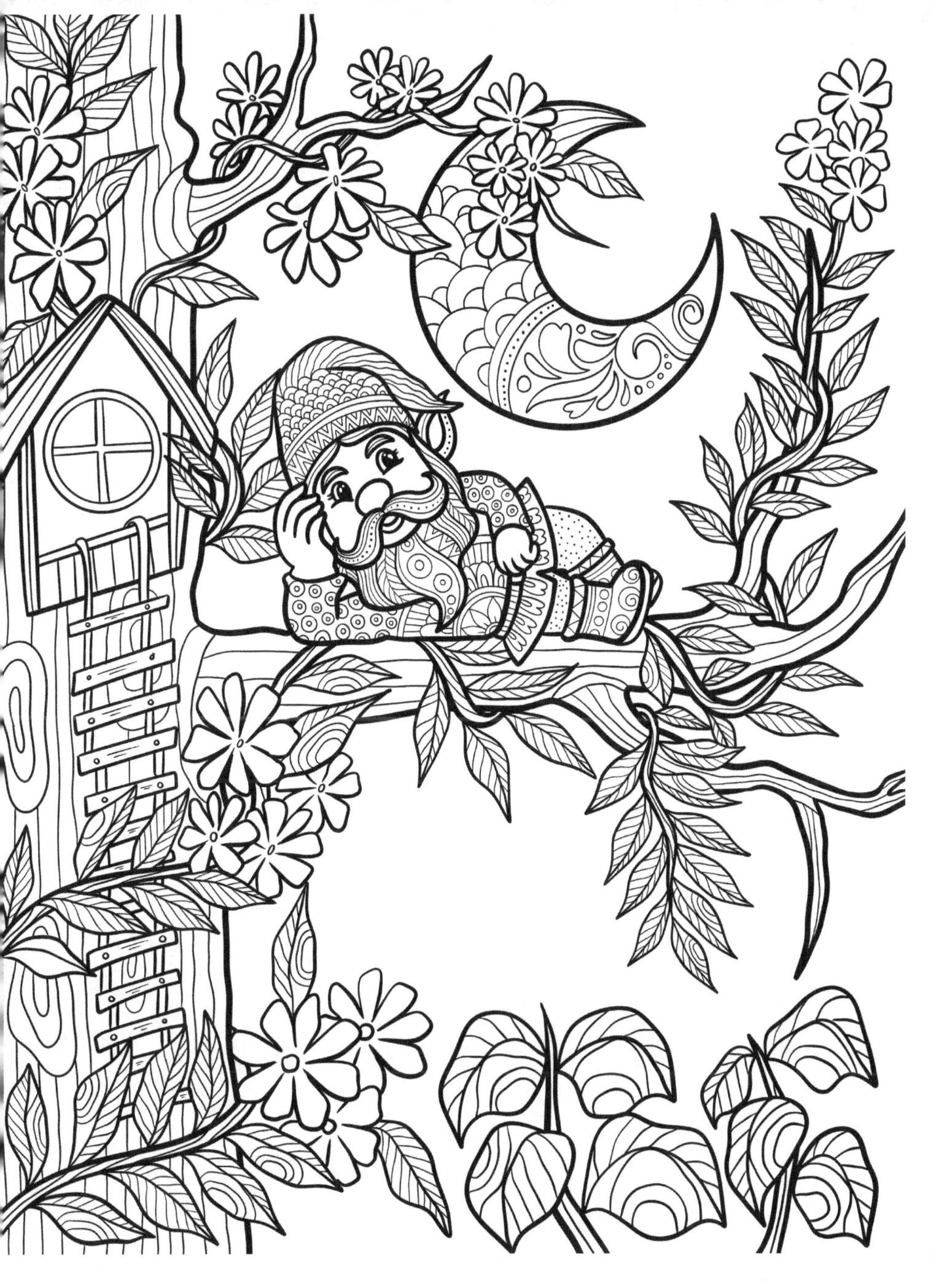

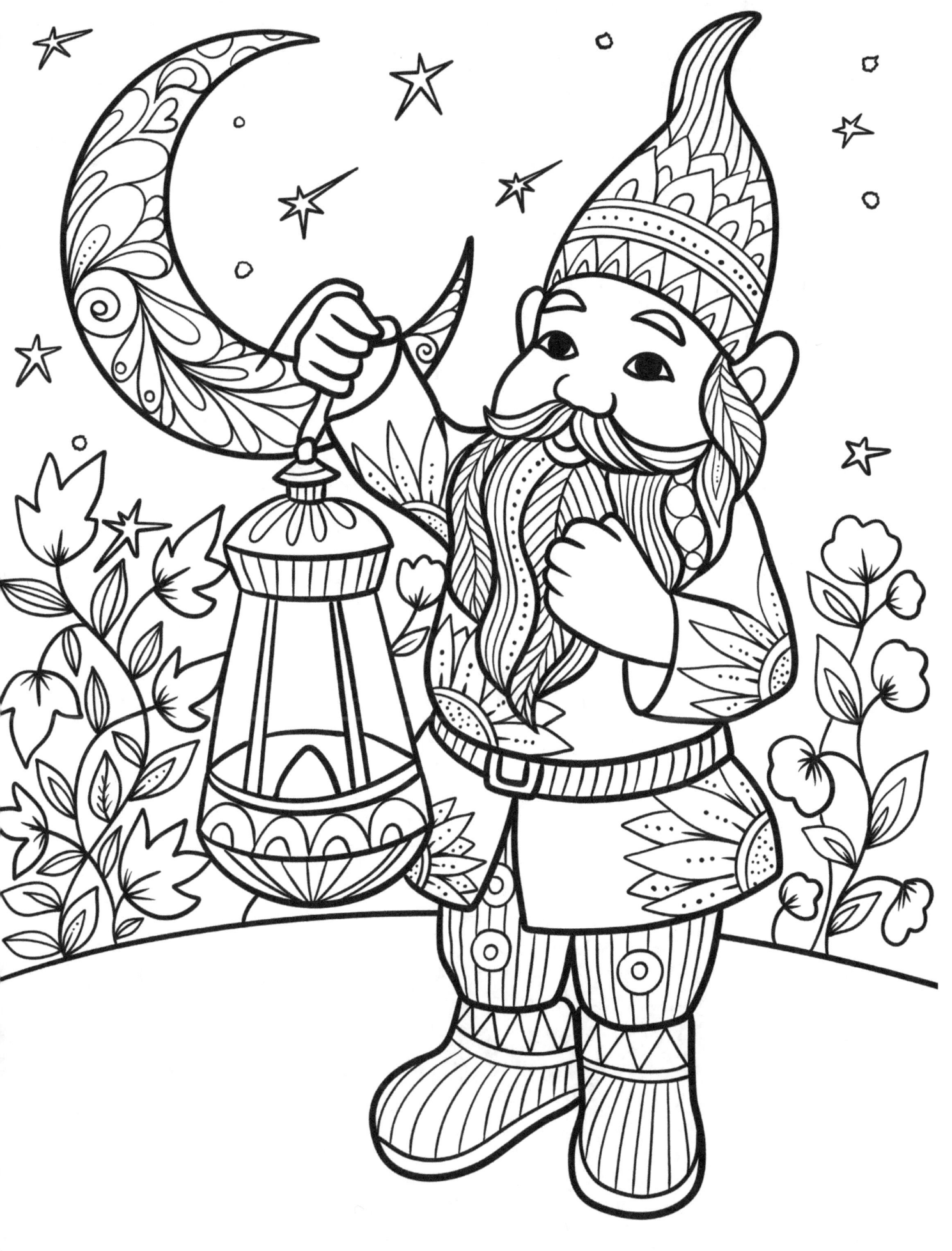

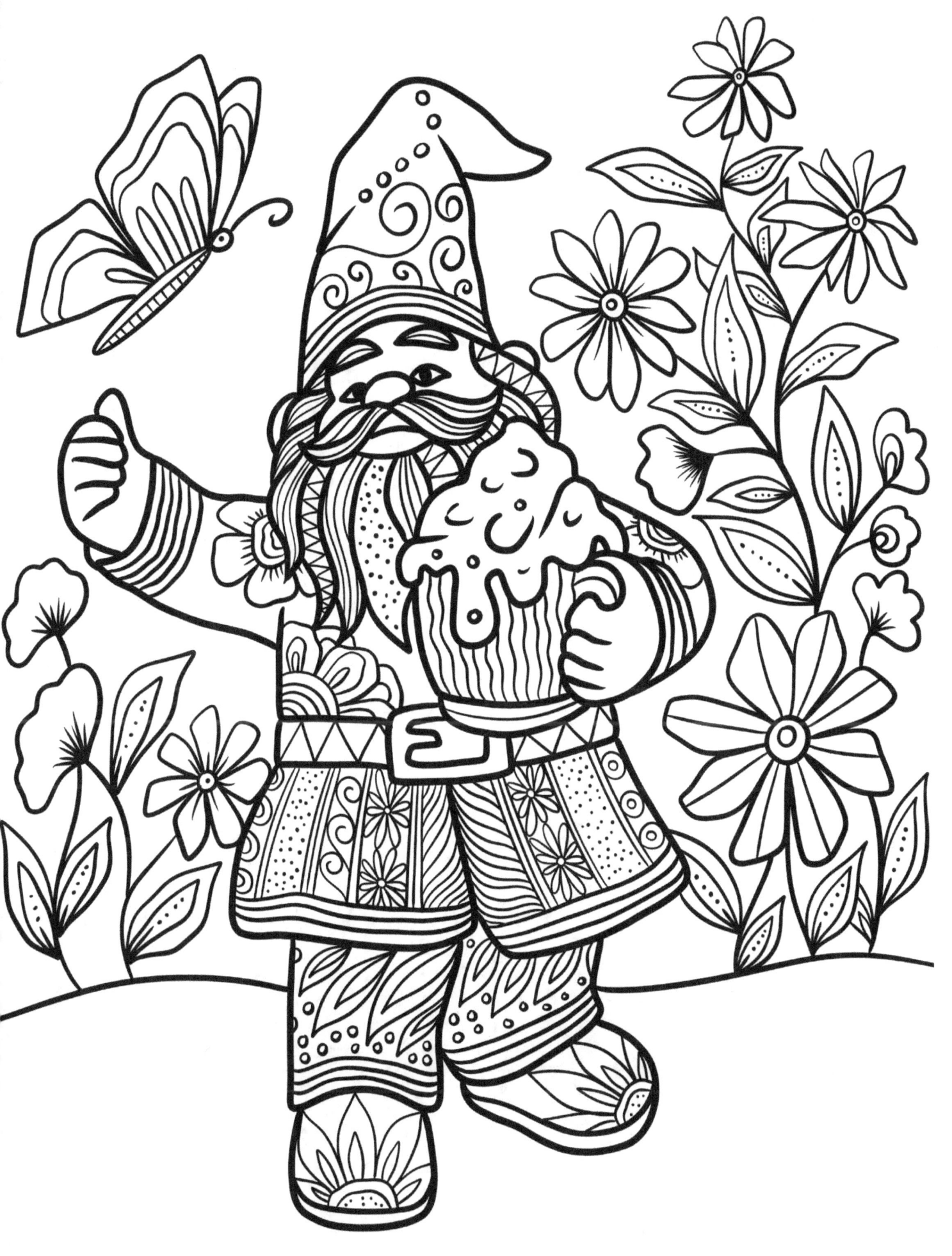

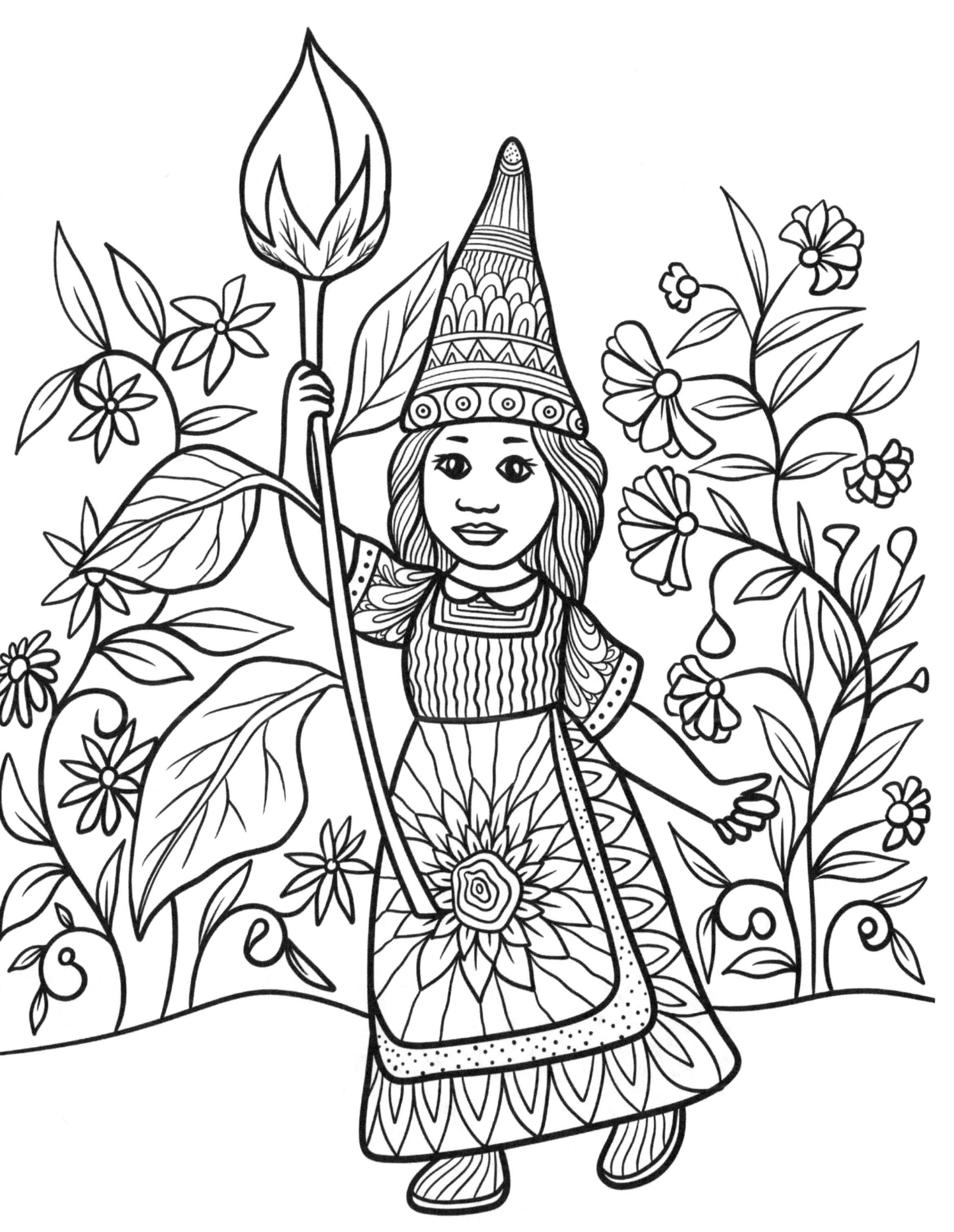

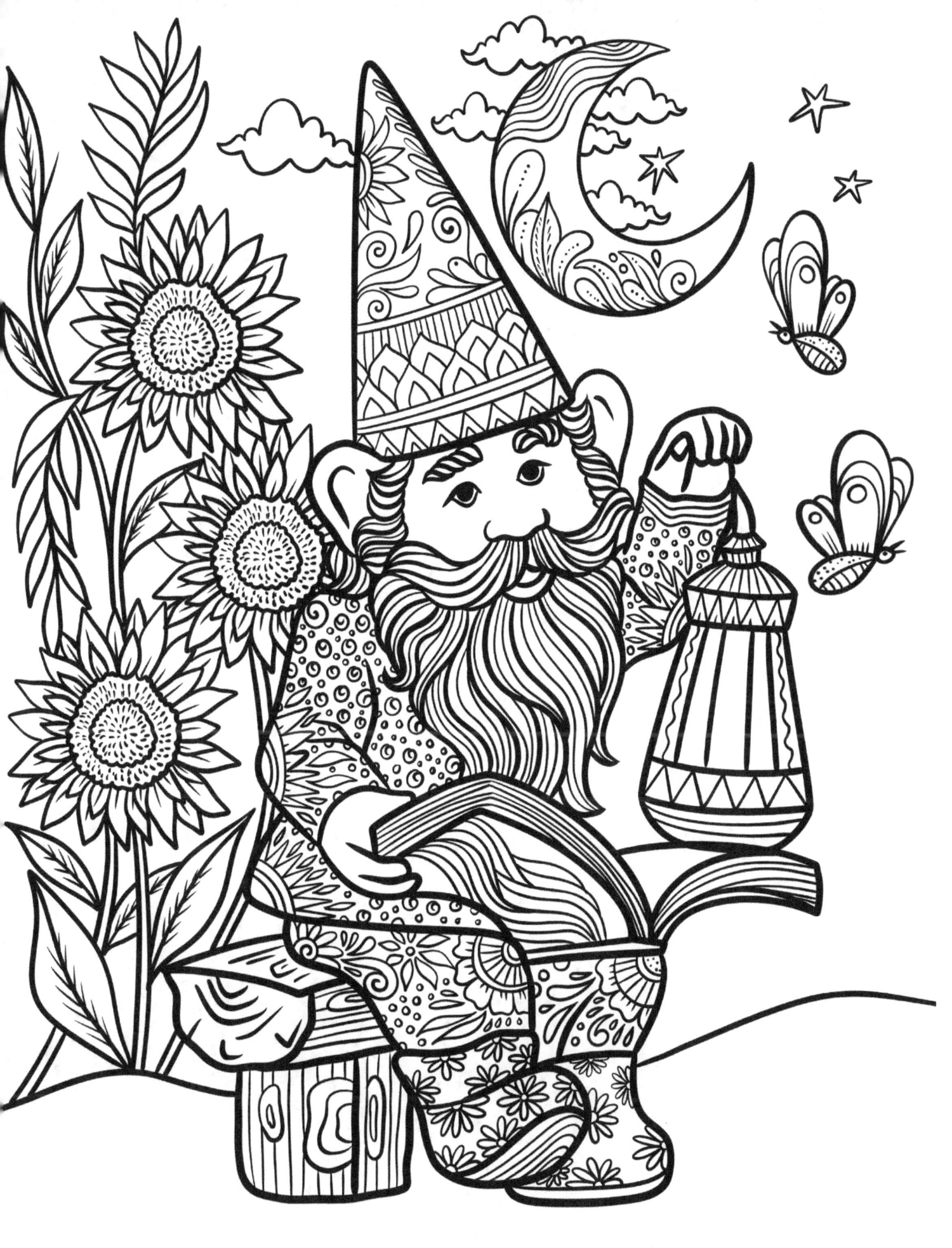

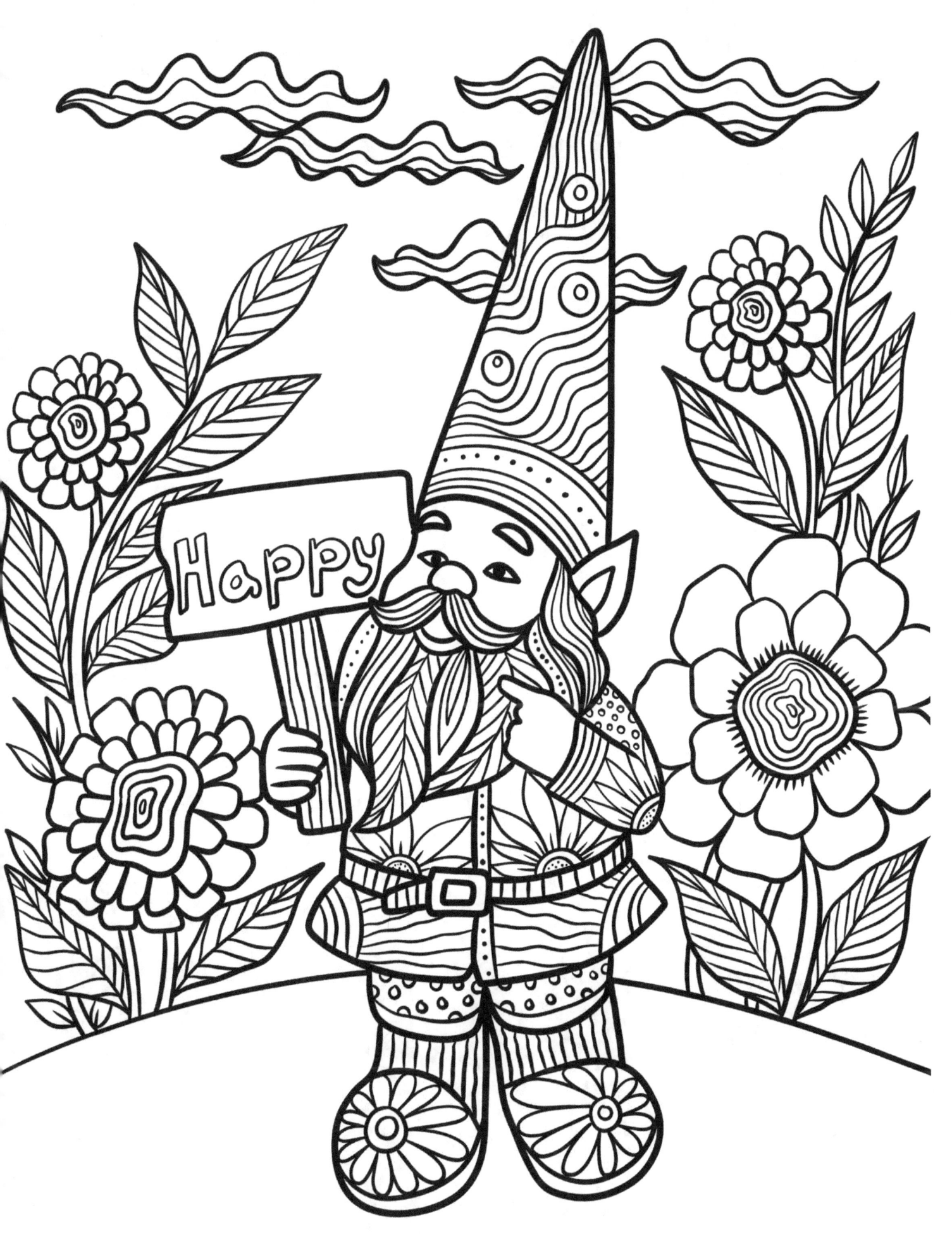

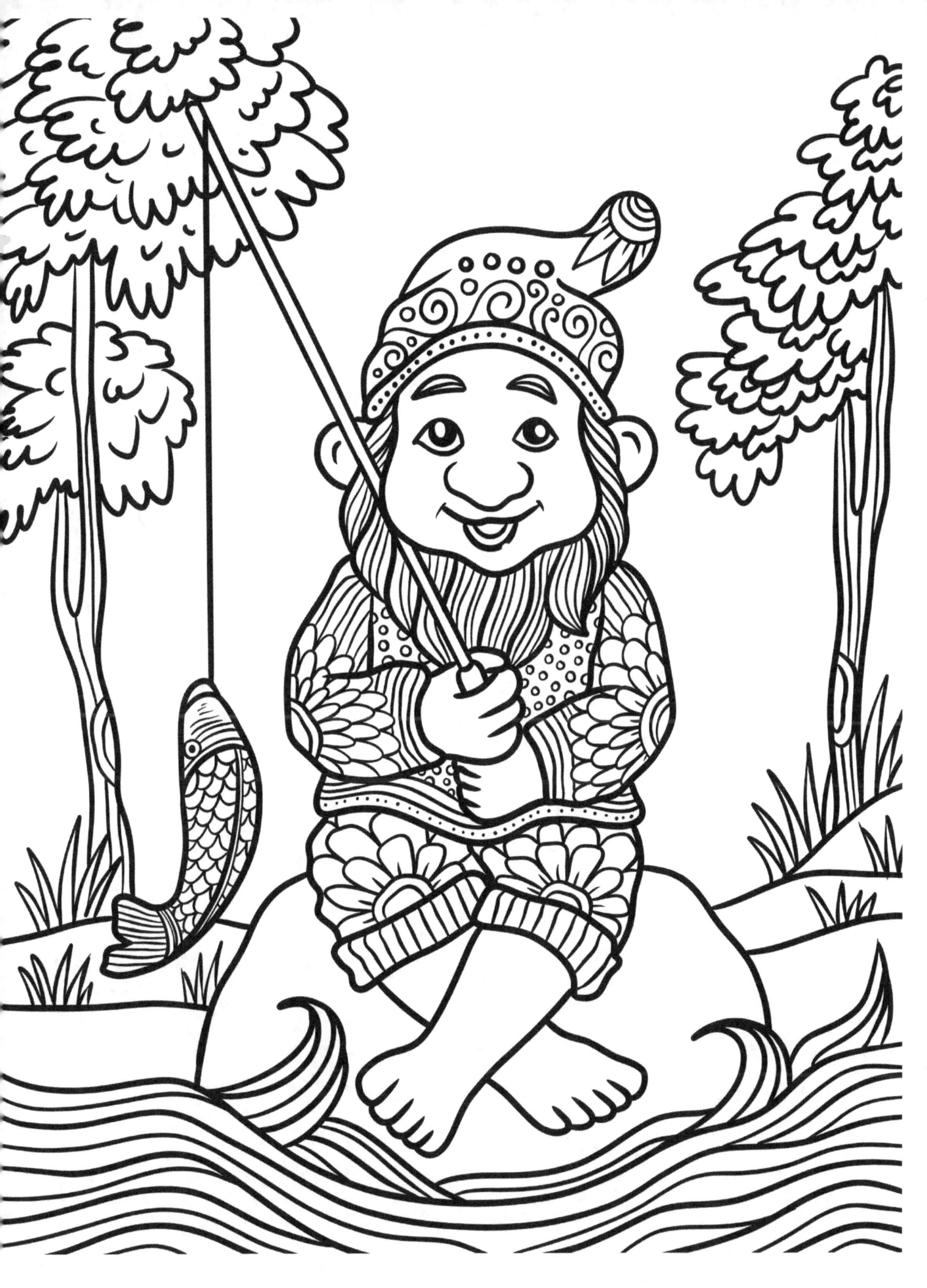

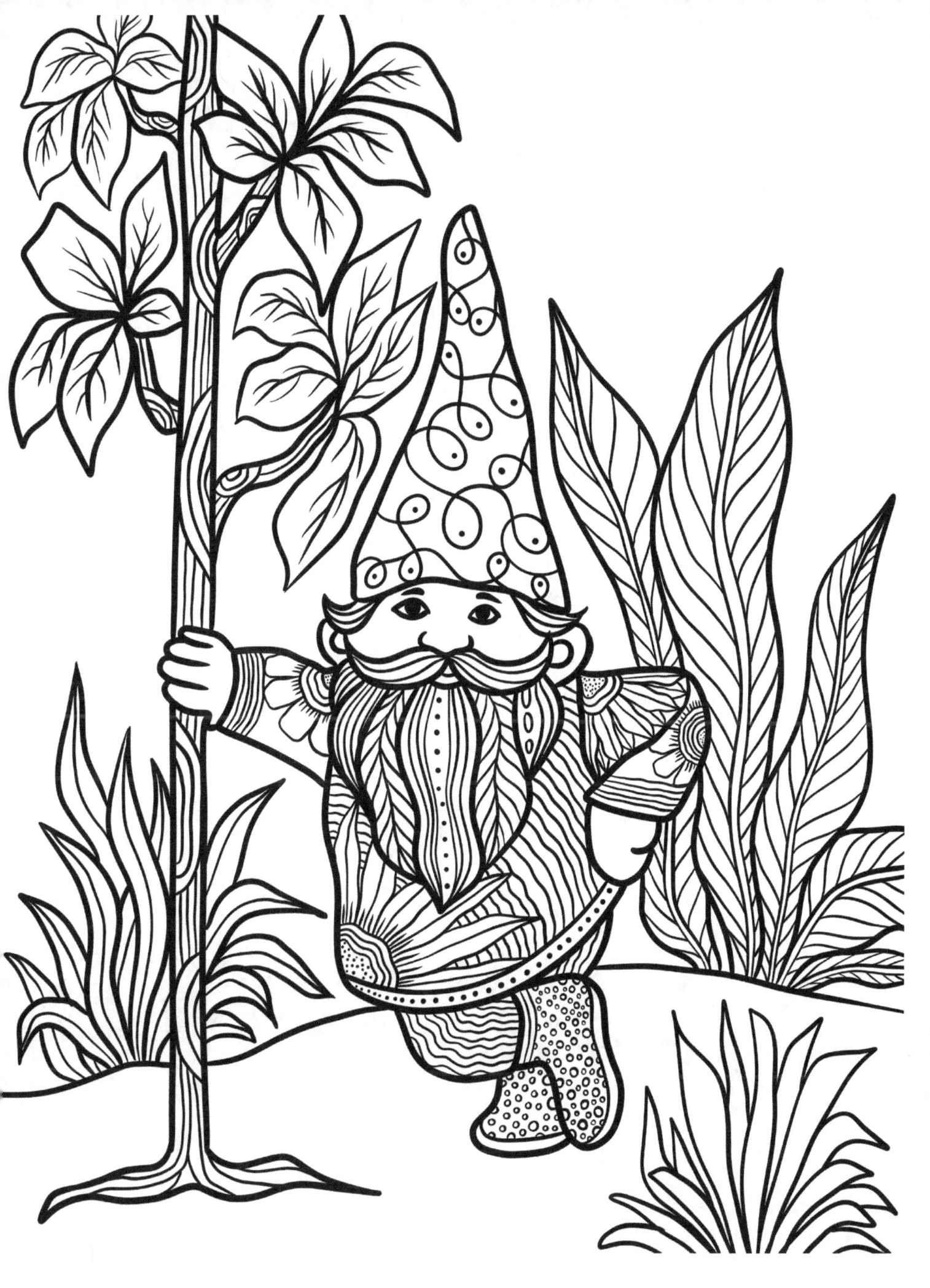

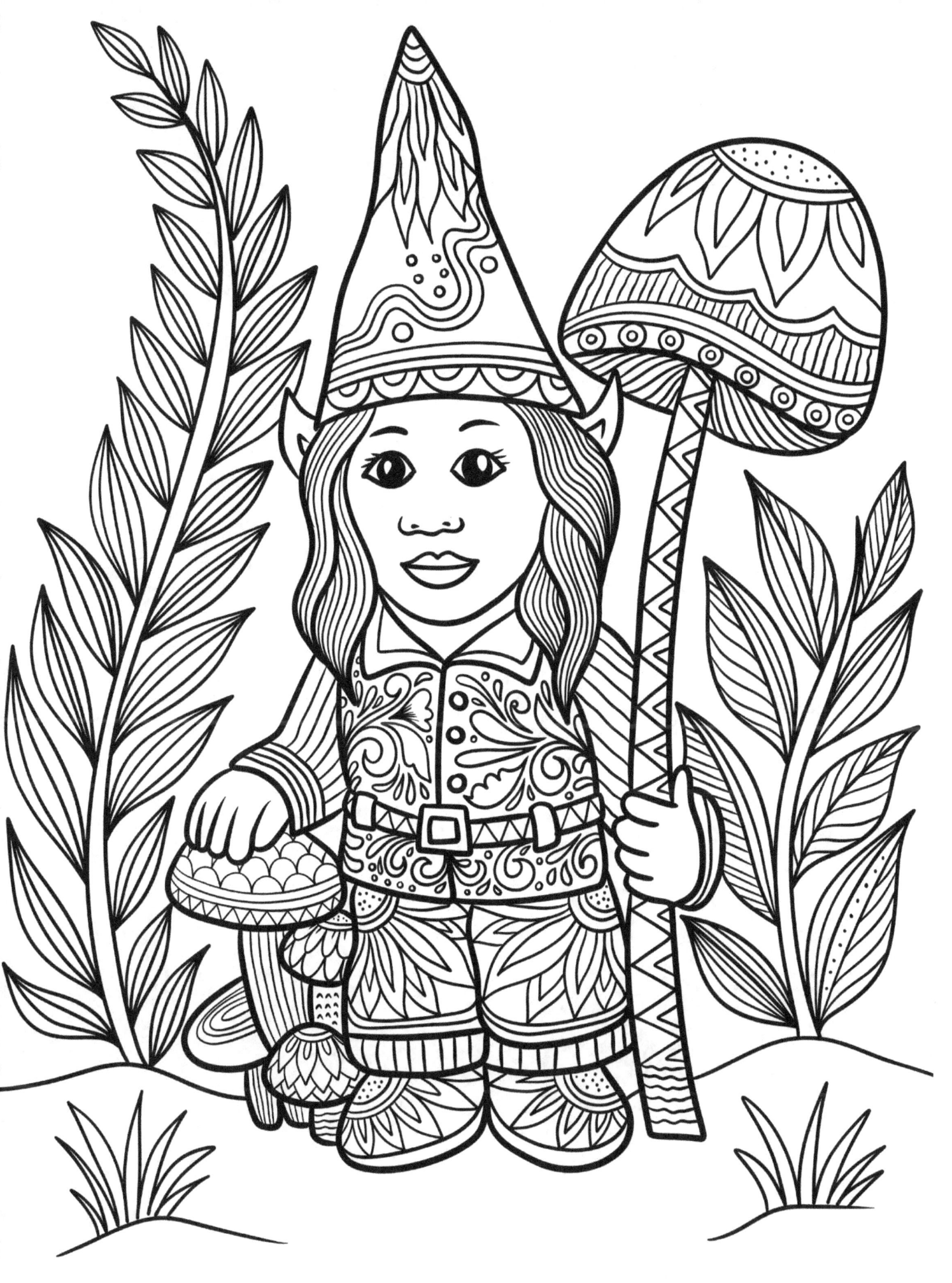

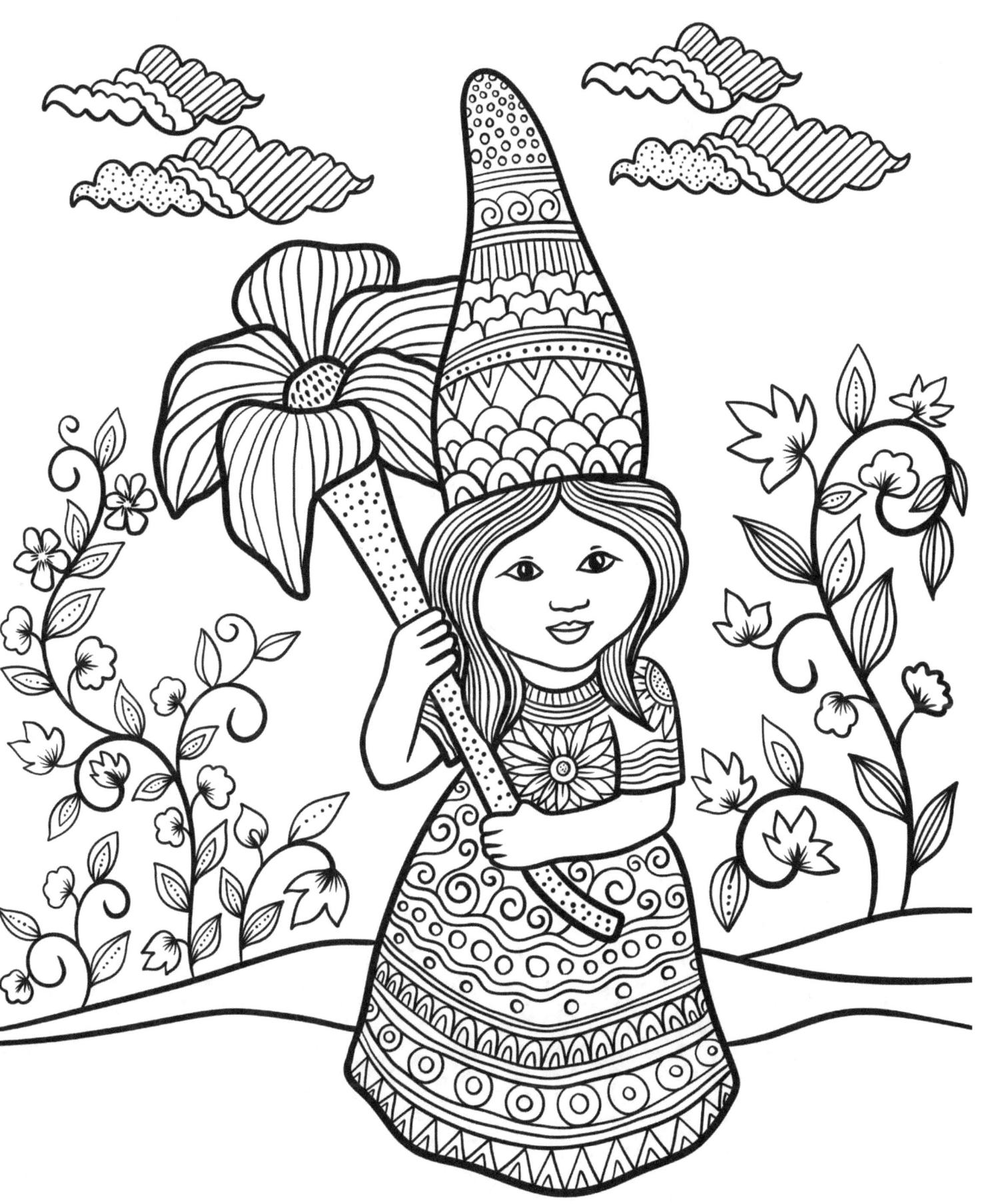

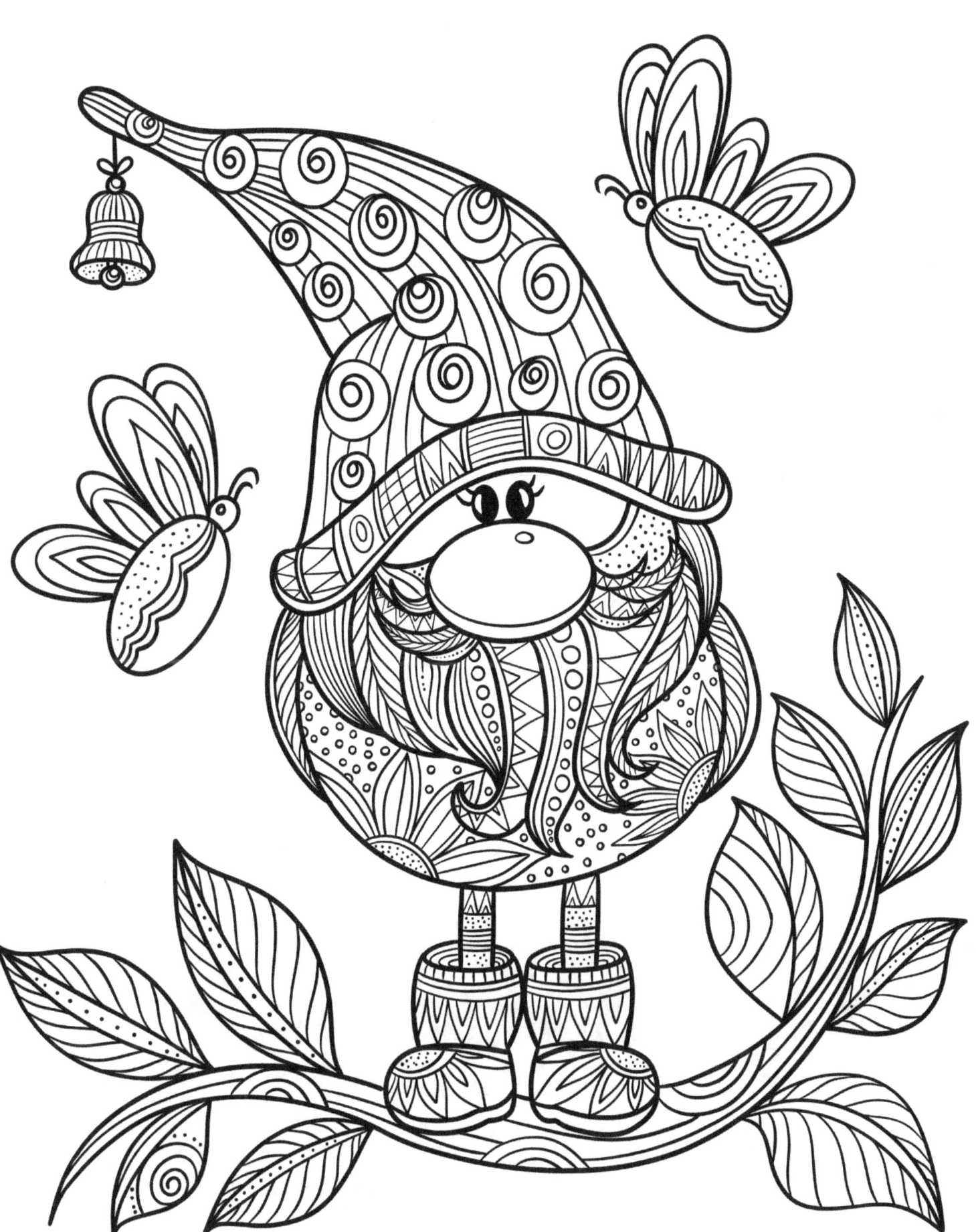

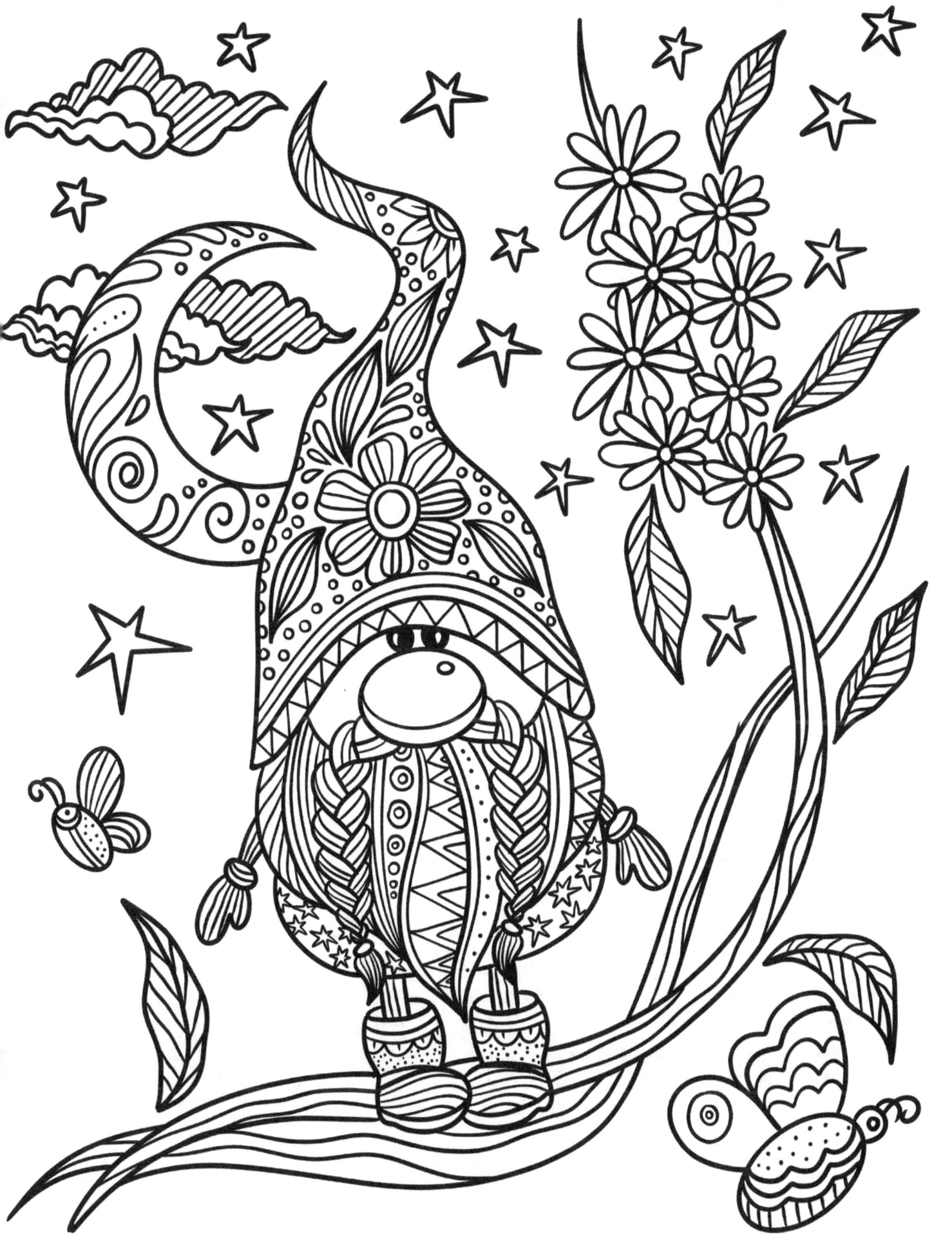

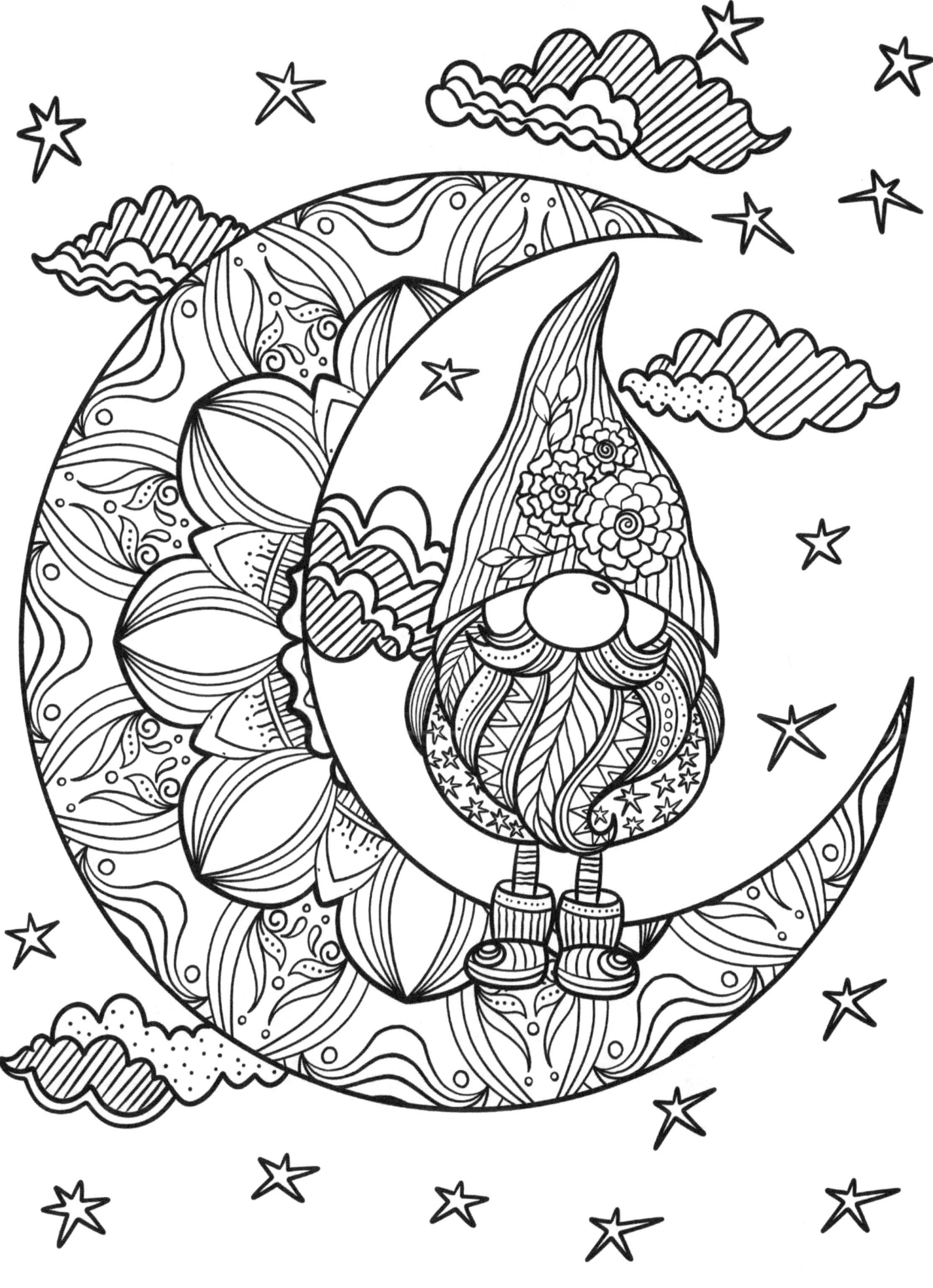

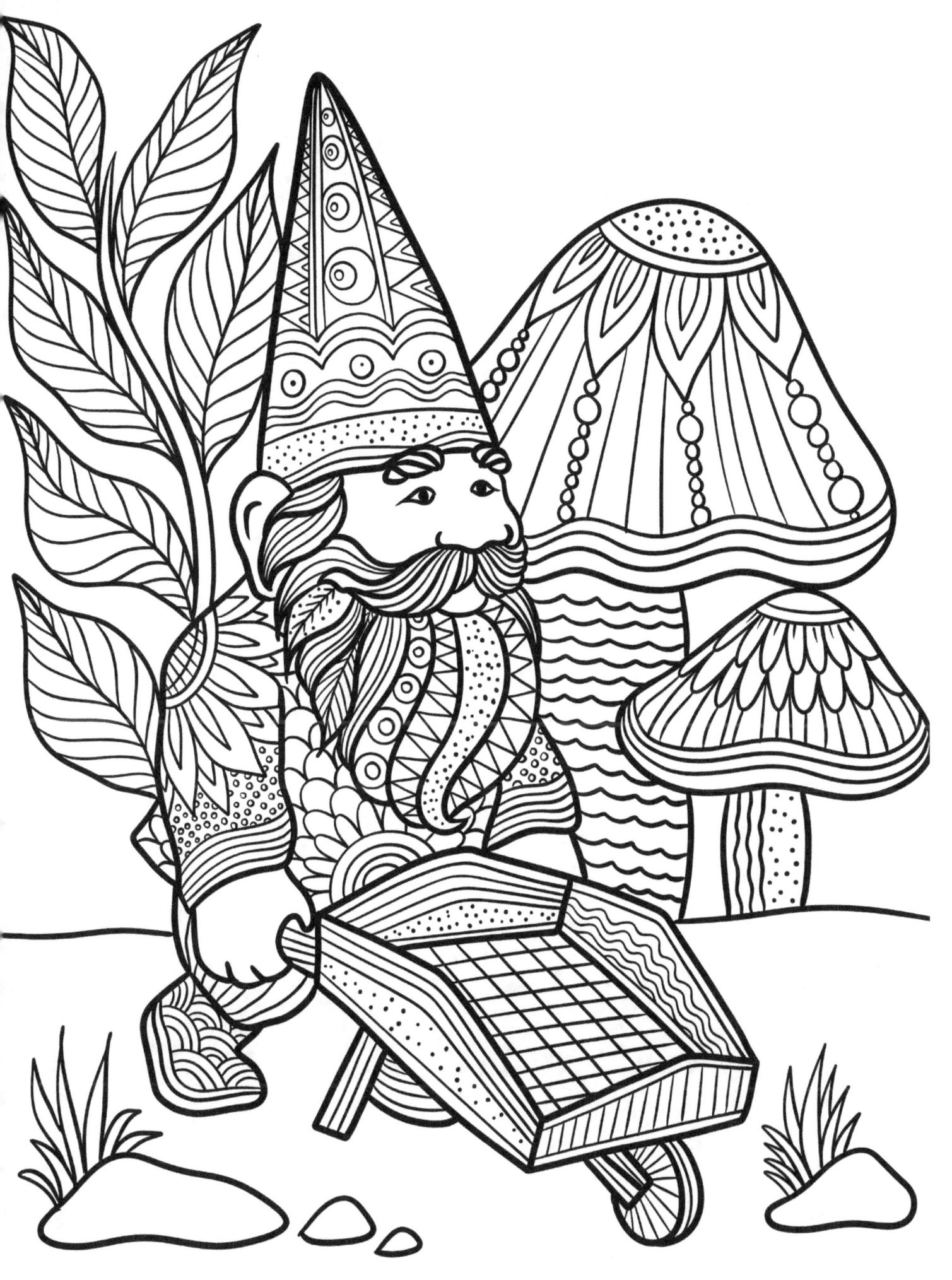

Thank you for purchasing this book.

If you would like to know more about
Aryla Publishing Books please visit:-

www.ArylaPublishing.com

Or follow us on
Facebook
Twitter
Instagram
for *free promotions*

@arylapublishing

We would love to know what you think of
this book so please leave us a review.

Have a wonderful day ☺

Other Coloring Books from Aryla Publishing

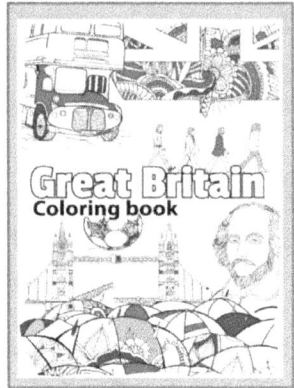
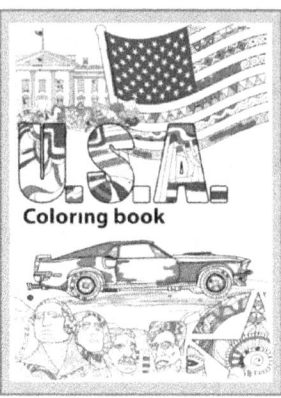
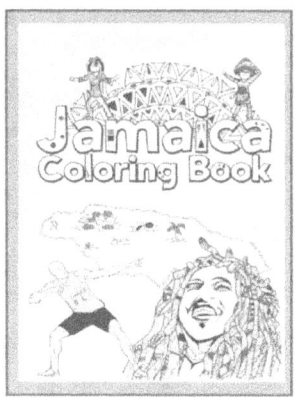
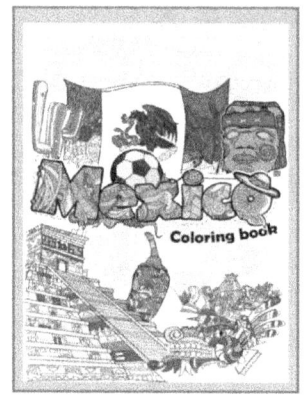

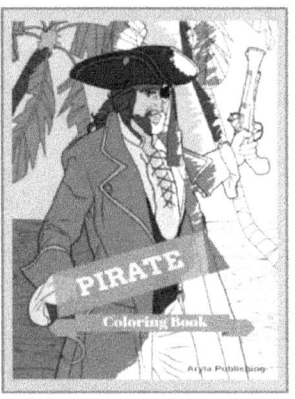
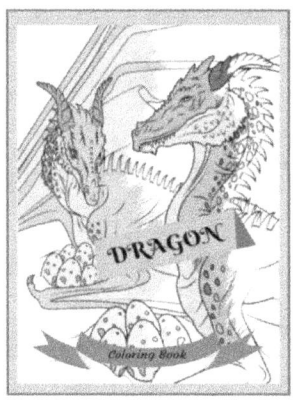
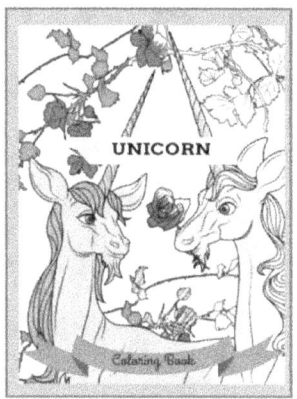
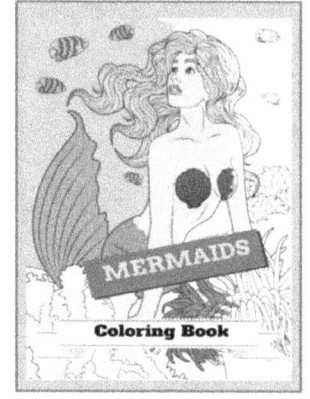

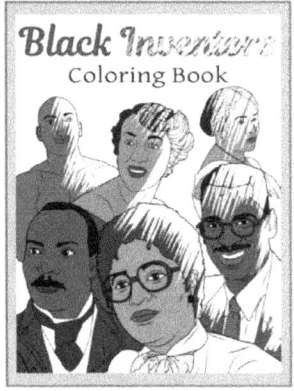
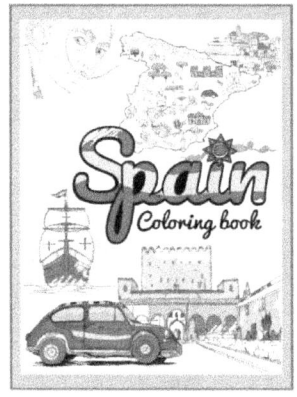
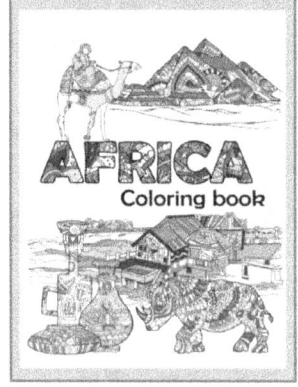
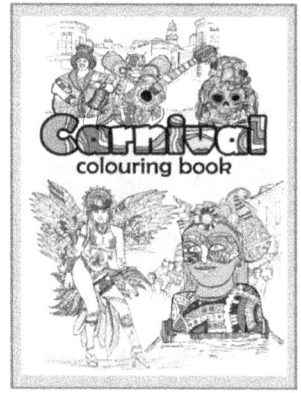

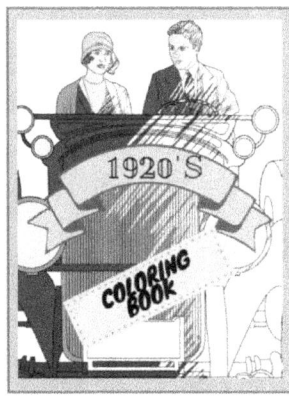
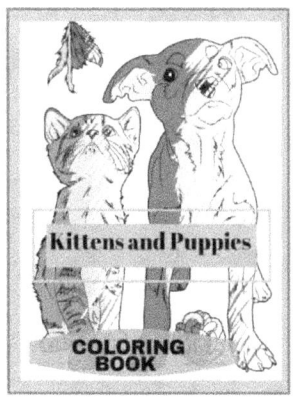
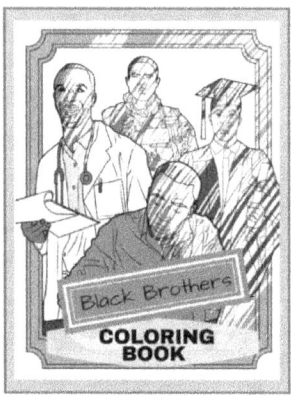
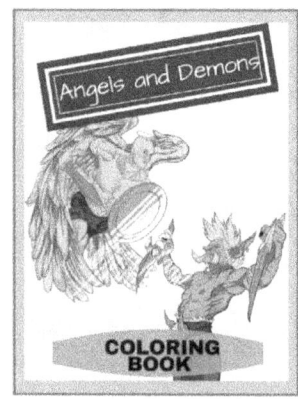

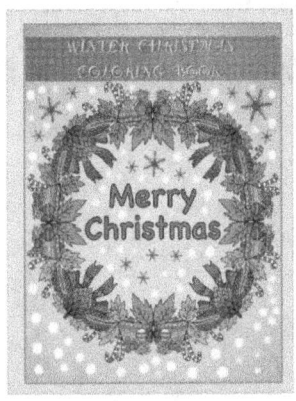
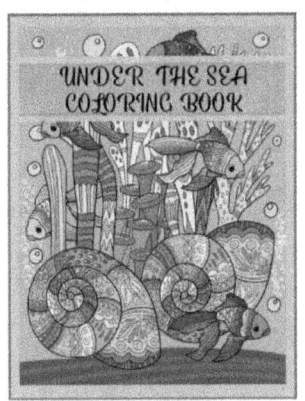
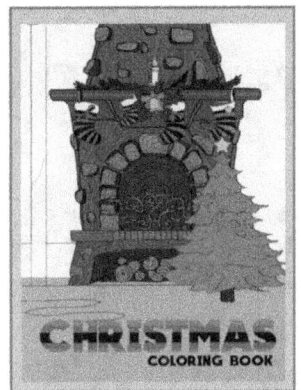
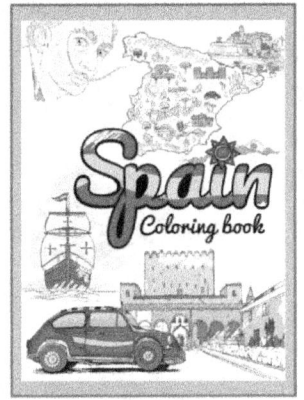
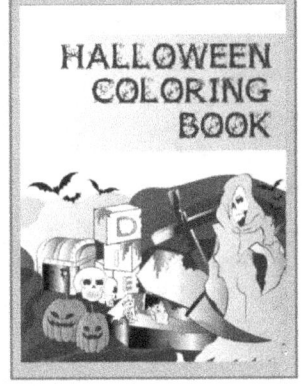
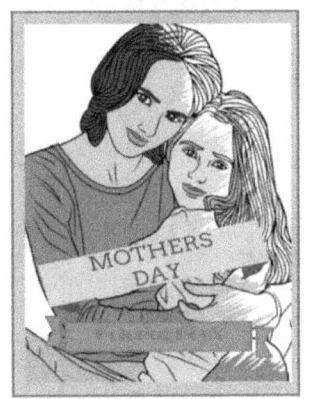
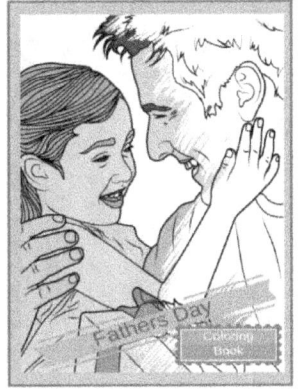
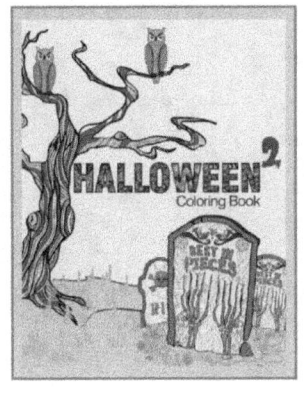
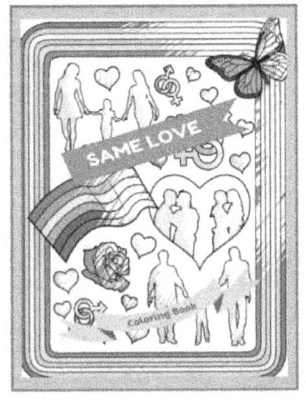
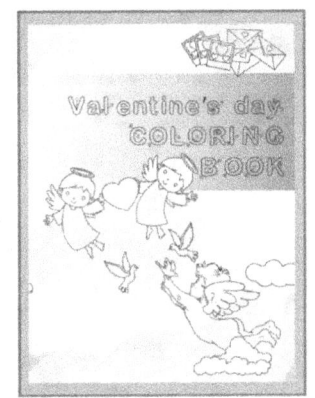
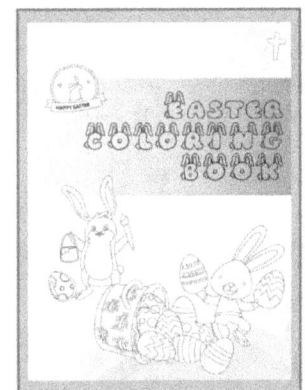
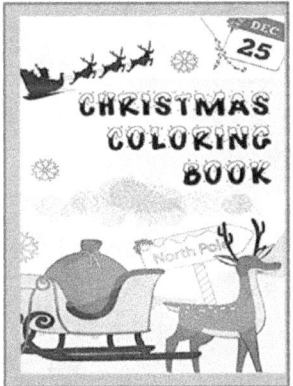
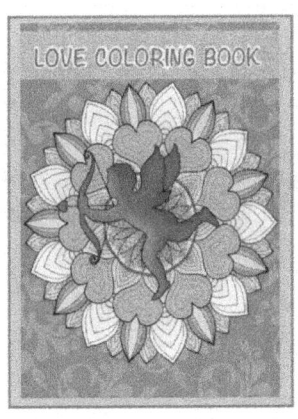
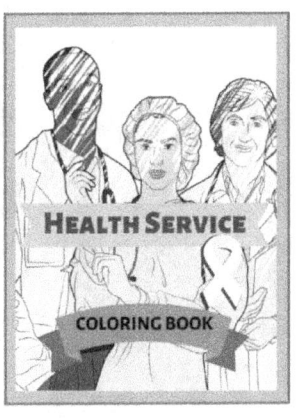
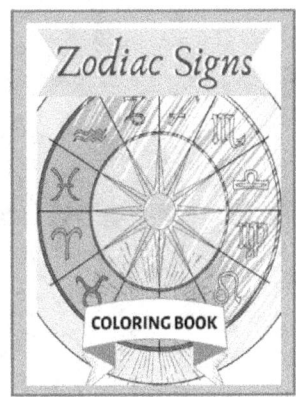
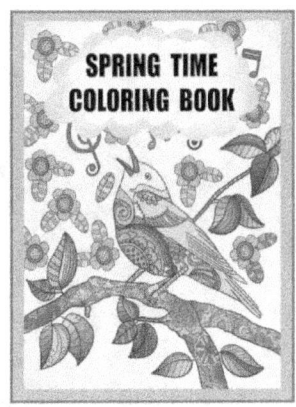

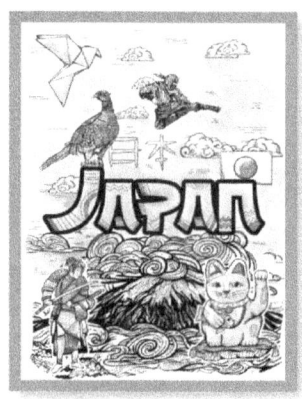

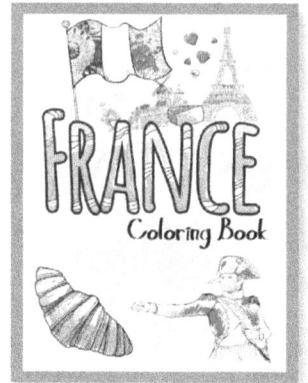

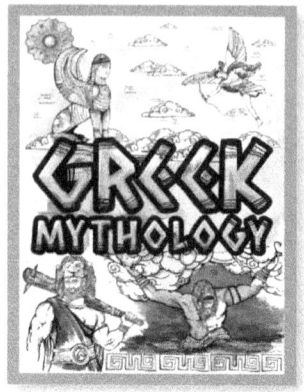

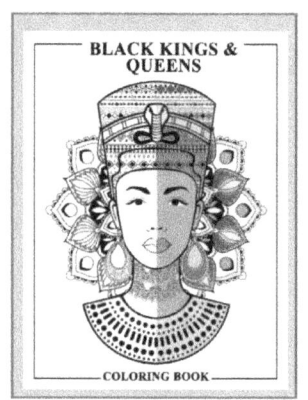

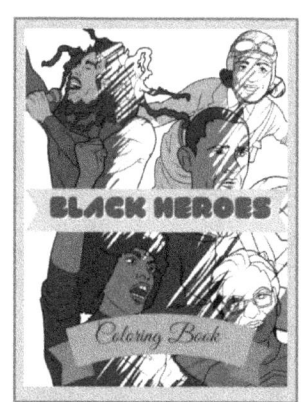

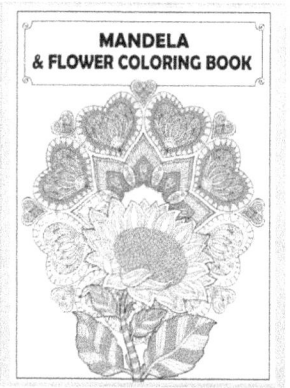

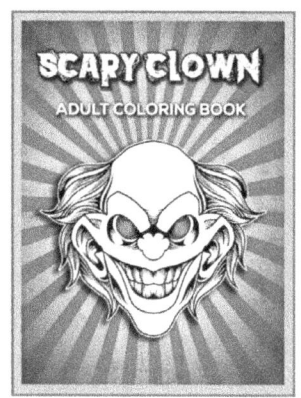

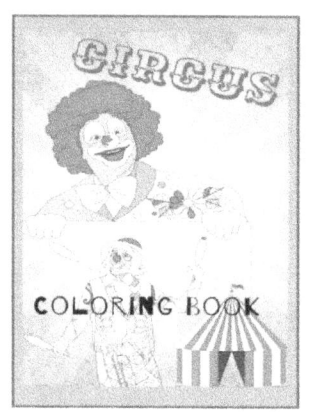

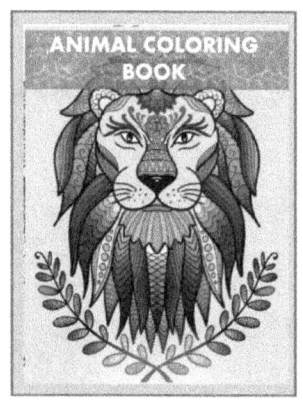

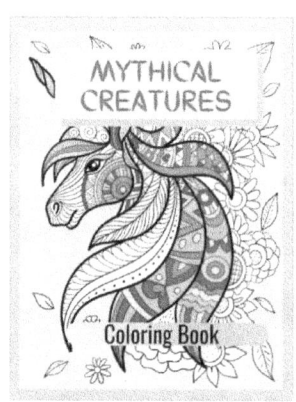

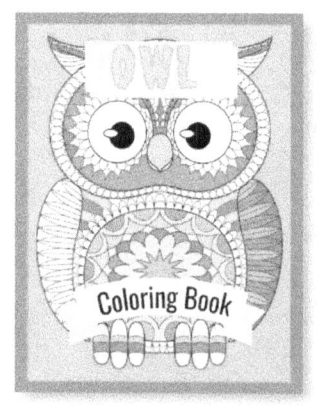

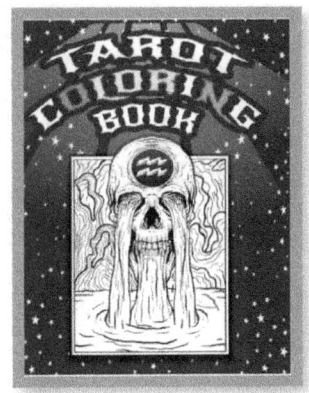

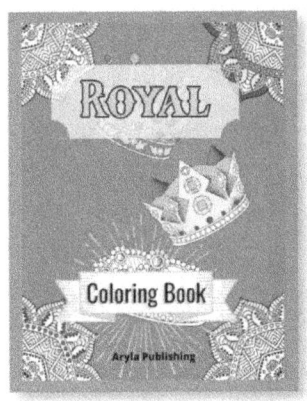

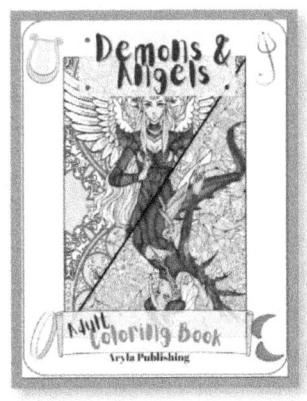

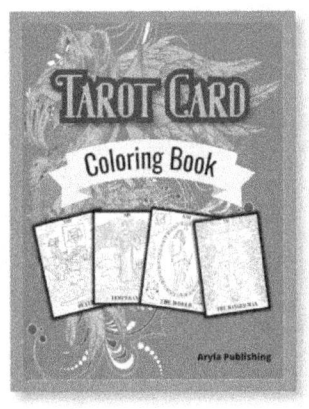

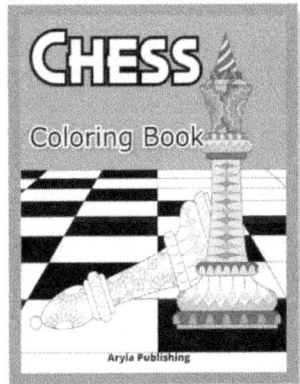

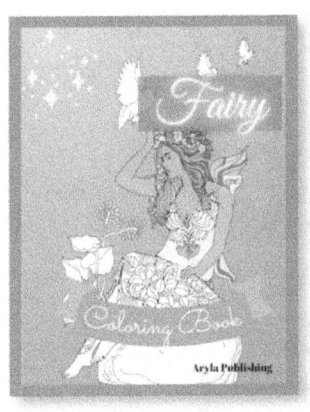

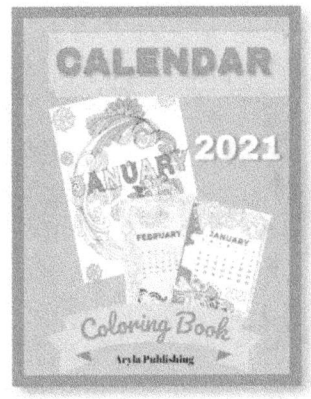

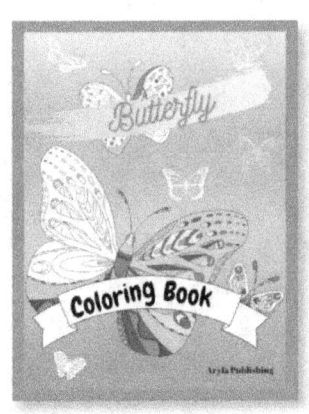

Color In Fun
Kids Books

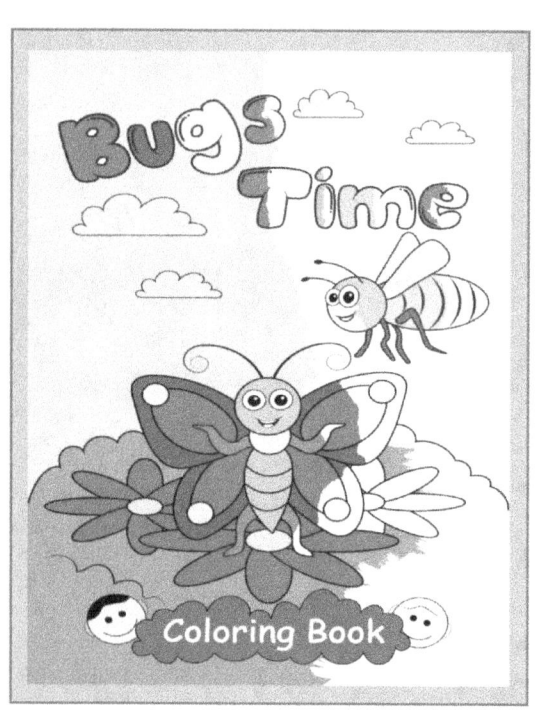

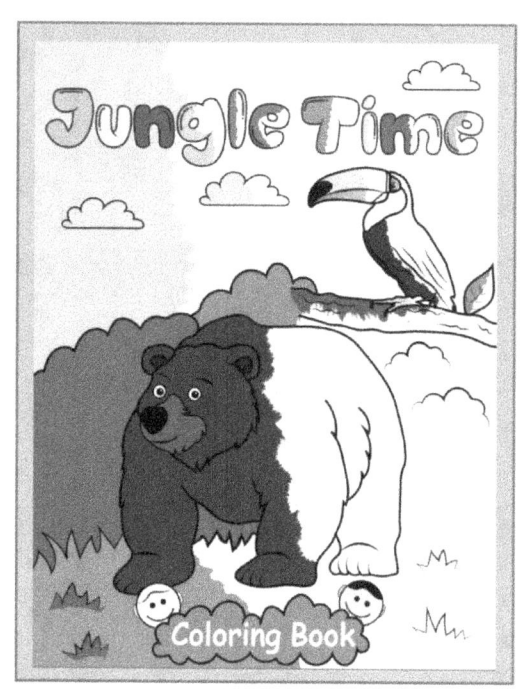

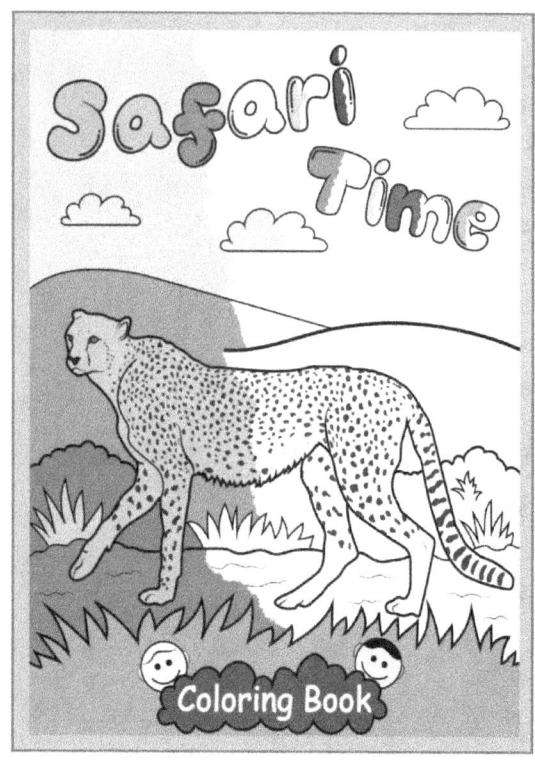

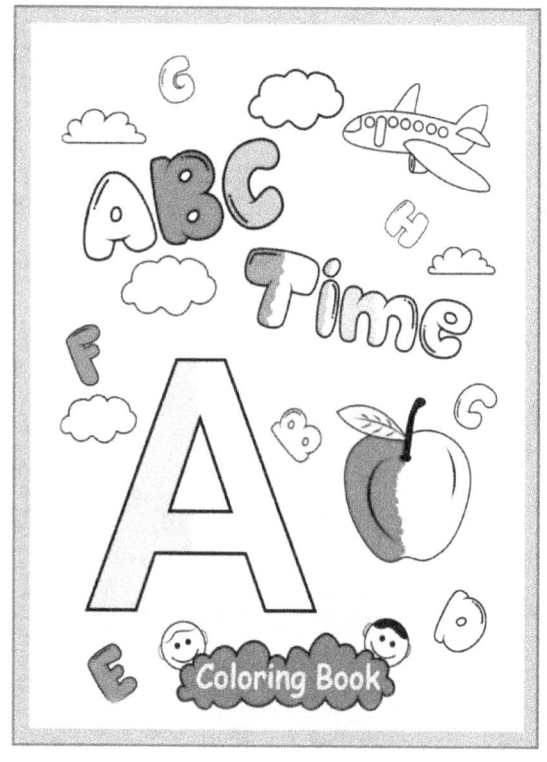

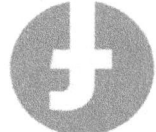  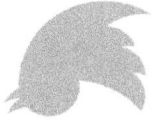